This book is dedicated to those brave men and women of the New York City Fire Department and The New York City Police Department, who risk their lives daily so that we may live in peace and safety.

Especially to those men and women who, without concern for personal safety, heroically gave their lives during the tragedy of September 11, 2001, a day which will live forever in the hearts and minds of all civilized people throughout the world.

Since I am native New Yorker, born and raised in Staten Island, I feel especially close to these events. Additionally, my family has had a long and proud history of serving the New York City Police Department. It began with my grandfather, the late Captain James F. Austin, who was one of the first bicycle patrol officers in 1917, became the youngest Lieutenant appointed in the city's history, and went on to command all three Staten Island police precincts before retiring.

Because of my deep connection to the NYPD, a portion of the proceeds from the sale of this book will be donated to the New York City Firefighters and Police Officer's Widows Fund.

Their brave acts will never be forgotten.

May God Bless them and their families and may they rest in peace.

Amen

RECLAIM YOUR LIFE

RECLAIM YOUR LIFE

How to Regain Your Happiness
Through Challenging Times

Jim Donovan

LAHASKA PUBLISHING
POST OFFICE BOX 1147
BUCKINGHAM, PA 18912

www.lahaskapublishing.com

ISBN: 0-96505348-2

Library of Congress Control Number: 2001119567

TABLE OF CONTENTS

INTRODUCTION

The time has come for you to reclaim your divine birth right to have a life of peace, joy happiness, excitement, health, love, prosperity, fun, passion and abundance. A life free from pain, struggle, lack and frustration.

Whether you are a parent, child, spouse, employer, professional, tradesperson, artist, baker, teacher or student, you owe it to yourself to make your life the best it can be.

The time has come for you to take back your power and create the life you deserve. The time has come for you to reclaim your life.

One of the major lessons learned on September 11, 2001 was that life is fragile and uncertain. You can either choose to live your life to the fullest–right now, making it everything it can be, or be one of those people Henry David Thoreau was talking about when he said, "The mass of men lead lives of quite desperation."

This little book contains simple, practical ideas to help you reclaim your life. Each 'mini" chapter has been carefully selected to help you regain a sense of purpose in your life and reclaim your happiness and joy.

Use the ideas in this book to help you reclaim your life. Examine the concepts, complete the exercises, take what works for you, and leave the rest. Be true to yourself, and above all, live your life to the fullest.

ACCEPTANCE

If you want to achieve happiness and live your life to the fullest, it is necessary to accept where you are and who you are, right now. This is an important first step in our growth and is the starting place for change to begin.

All too often we look at a situation, decide how we think it should be and act on our perception of it. The problem with this is that it is pure fantasy. If all we do is wish things were different, we will wind up constantly being frustrated.

We must learn to accept circumstances as they are, not as we would like them to be.

How many times have you said, "If only things were like the good old days, then I'd be happy"?

There is a wonderful little prayer, the Serenity Prayer, which can remind us to be more accepting:

God grant me the
Serenity to accept the things I cannot change,
Courage to change the things I can,
Wisdom to know the difference.

You cannot change circumstances but you can change how you react to them. It is important to know the difference between the two.

ACCEPT YOURSELF

The second part of acceptance is learning to accept ourselves as we are in this moment. We sabotage ourselves by saying things like "if only I had more money" or "if I were ten pounds lighter, then . . ."

We cannot change what is! We can, however, accept everything about ourselves, warts and all, right here and right now. Then, and only then, can we begin to make the changes we desire and become the person we are capable of becoming. By accepting ourselves right here and right now, we will be less likely to allow occasional setbacks to divert us from our goals.

When I talk about denial, I'm not talking about the river in Africa. I'm talking about being 50 pounds overweight and rationalizing it by telling yourself you have "big bones." Are your bones really big or are you simply overweight from eating too much and not exercising?

Accept yourself as you are right now – good or bad. Be honest with yourself and acknowledge where you are.

Surrender The Illusion

If you want to change your life in any way, you must first face the reality of your life as it is right now. You have to be willing to stop living an illusion of what you think your life is.

This truth became really clear to me one sunny morning in April, 1986. I was coming out of deep sleep and, as I opened one eye on that sunny spring day, my head was throbbing from yet another night of too much partying. Nothing new there. My life had become one big party, or so I thought. The reality was that my life was out of control and had spiralled all the way down to what was to be my personal bottom.

As I opened my eye, I noticed one of those little smiley faces. You know the kind, the little stickers with a smiley face on them. I thought this was kind of strange as I tried to get my bearings and clear the fog in my head. I then noticed that the smiley face was on a pair of slippers that were attached to my feet.

I began looking around at the surroundings. It was a bleak looking room with pale green walls, overhead neon lights- with a dull flicker and hospital beds around me. I immediately knew I was not at the Four Seasons.

I was, as I would learn later, in the Alcohol Detox ward at a local hospital. That was the beginning of my accepting my reality. I had hit my own personal bottom. There I was in a hospital, friendless, penniless, homeless, jobless, at the bottom of my life. I was mentally, spiritually, physically and financially bankrupt.

The interesting thing is that this was also a major turning point in my life. I knew I had to change my life. I had to surrender and decide right then and there to change or die.

I had to decide to make some major changes in my life if I wanted to reclaim my own life. During the few days I spent in the hospital, I had plenty of time to think about my life. I vowed to accept the help that was being offered and do whatever it took to have my once promising life back.

The best way I know to begin this, or any personal change, is to take an inventory of your life as it is this very moment. This will help you determine those areas where you want to make changes. Be sure to devote some time completing the exercise on the following page. Find a quiet place where you will not be disturbed and really examine your life. By the way, this is a good exercise to do from time to time as your life changes.

MY PERSONAL INVENTORY

To become clearer about the changes you want to make, complete the following exercise. In your journal, draw six headings, for each of the six major areas of your life listed below:

- Family/social
- Career/business
- Health/fitness
- Spiritual/emotional
- Money/finances
- Mental/educational

Under each heading, write what it is you would like to change or work on improving. For example, if you are overweight and have health challenges, write that under "Health/Fitness." If your income is not what you would like it to be, write "increase income" under "Financial."

Don't forget to also list the things you like about yourself along with those you want to change. We have a tendency to overlook the good parts of ourselves. We all have attributes we like and it is important not to forget about these. Sure, there are probably lots of characteristics you would like to change but give yourself a pat on the back for the parts that you are satisfied with. Come back to this list from time to time to gauge your progress.

> *"If it's to be, it's up to me"*
> ANTHONY ROBBINS

TAKING RESPONSIBILITY FOR YOUR OWN LIFE

Now that you have taken an inventory of your present state of affairs, the next step in creating the life you want to have is taking responsibility for all of your "stuff."

If you listen to a group of people talking, you immediately realize we live in a society that is built on blaming outside forces for the conditions in our lives. People point to the government as the reason they are not happy, or their bosses, spouses, lack of education, the economy, the school system, and the currently most popular dumping ground — the dysfunctional family. They point to everyone but themselves.

The problem with this kind of attitude is that it completely takes away our personal power to make changes. Think about it. If the cause of unhappiness or a lack of prosperity in my life is something outside of my own area of control, then how can I possibly expect to change it? If I am broke because of something the government did, then I am stuck there! Regardless of how much we look to outside forces to solve our problems, we are always 100% accountable for our lives.

On the other hand, if I take complete responsibility for the conditions in my life, I then have the power to do something about them. This may sound like an oversimplification or merely a play on words but it is a critical distinction. We must take responsibility for everything presently in our lives. Whether or not we believe we "caused" them in our conscious or subconscious minds is irrelevant. The fact is we have these situations in our lives, and if we see that we somehow contributed to their being there, we are then empowered to make changes.

If, for instance, you blame your lack of education for not having the kind of job you want, then you are stuck right where you are. On the other hand, if you accept responsibility for this lack of education, you can do something in the present to change it. Perhaps you could go back to school, take a correspondence course, study on your own or whatever. The point is that once you take responsibility, you are empowered to make changes. Remember that the point of power is always in the present moment. At any given time in our lives, we can choose to change. It is important to recognize that, while we may move forward and backward, we do not become "stuck" in the powerless position of blaming outside forces for the conditions in our lives.

Begin now to take responsibility for creating the life you want. As has been suggested– make your life a work of art in progress.

WILLINGNESS

If you talk to anyone who has overcome an addiction, you will learn that they first had to become willing to go to any lengths to get the help they needed. The people who have been successful were willing. In some cases, this meant moving to another state, changing jobs, or in extreme cases, leaving their families. Whatever it took, the people who succeeded were willing.

While you may not have an addiction to deal with, no doubt you have some changes you wish to make. The key to your success is your willingness. This does not mean you will necessarily have to take drastic steps, but that you must be willing to do whatever is necessary to accomplish what you want in your life.

If, for instance, you want a new career or a better job, perhaps you must become willing to go back to school and get the necessary education in order to change jobs. If you want a better relationship with your family, you may have to be willing to become more flexible in your demands. If you want to be able to take walks on the beach and you live in Kansas, you must be willing to move or accept some different type of experience to give you pleasure.

Ask yourself what you must become willing to do to make the necessary changes, what you must become willing to learn and what you must become willing to change to have what you want.

It is important to become willing and to make the commitment to change. Based on your personal inventory exercise, list one or two changes you'd like to make:

- WHAT MUST YOU DO, RIGHT NOW, TO BEGIN THE CHANGE YOU WANT TO MAKE?

- WHAT DO YOU NEED TO LEARN? WHAT NEW SKILLS DO YOU NEED?

- WHAT NEEDS TO CHANGE FOR YOU TO MAKE PROGRESS ?

> *"Whether you think you can or you think you can't, you are right"*
>
> HENRY FORD

CREATE A STRONG BELIEF IN YOURSELF

Your beliefs about yourself and your capabilities will determine the quality of your life. It's quite simple. What you believe will dictate what you attempt to do, which will, in turn, determine what you experience. If you want to have a full, satisfying life, you'll want to create a strong belief about your possibilities and your ability to have the kind of life you want.

In the course of studying success and successful people, I have uncovered several characteristics shared by virtually all people who have become highly successful. One of the primary characteristics they all share is a belief in themselves and their ability to succeed. Successful people are that way because of the beliefs they hold about themselves. Successful people expect to succeed. Unsuccessful people do not. It's that simple.

You too can develop and strengthen your beliefs in yourself and your ability to succeed in whatever you do. Eliminate doubt and uncertainty from your life. Avoid asking questions like, "What if I fail?" or "What if it does not work?" The very act of asking questions such as these will create doubt in your mind and weaken your belief in yourself.

Instead, ask empowering questions like, "What is the best way to do this and ensure my success?" Or you might ask, "How could I best achieve the results I am seeking?"

Tell yourself over and over that you can do it. Use visualization and mental pictures to see yourself achieving a successful outcome in whatever you attempt. Think back in your life to times when you were successful and replay those events in your mind. This will help boost your self-confidence and affirm your belief in your own abilities. Get rid of phrases like; I'll try, I hope I can, and I think I can do it.

Instead, replace them with affirmative statements such as I will do it, I will succeed, I can do it. The more you reinforce and strengthen your internal beliefs, the more likely you are to succeed. Become an "I can" person, and as the commercial says, "Just do it." Remember the words of the great American inventor, Thomas Edison, who said, "If we did all the things we are capable of doing, we would literally astonish ourselves.

"Change can either challenge or threaten us. Your beliefs pave your way to success or block you."

MARSHA SINETAR

LEARN TO EMBRACE CHANGE

If there's one thing we can count on in our lives, it's that everything that is happening now will change! We live in an ever-changing universe. Everything in our world, including our very bodies, is changing. The cells in your body are totally replaced every seven years.

The seasons change as do governments, businesses, cultures, the sun, the moon, the stars, and of course, us. As a matter of fact, the only constant in our universe, is change.

For some reason, it is our nature to resist change of any kind. We waste precious time and energy attempting to resist change while living in a universe that is changing constantly.

What is it about human beings that makes us so willing to stay in an unhealthy situation just because it is familiar to us? Why would we rather remain in a dead end job, continue in a destructive relationship, or stay "stuck" in a lifestyle we dislike simply because we are in a "comfort zone" of familiarity? Is the fear of change so strong that we are willing to allow our lives to slip quietly by rather than face our fears and make the changes to improve our situation? If you are tired of being "stuck" and are ready to face your fear, you can begin by developing a new belief that says, "Change is good!" If you look back over your life and examine those times when you were forced to make changes, you will find that, when all was said and done, the outcome was positive and your life was enriched by having made the change.

The fear associated with venturing into the unknown, whether it be in a new job, a new relationship, moving to a new city, or simply making changes in your daily routine, is perfectly normal and is to be expected. While it is normal to associate a certain amount of fear and apprehension to making changes, it is destructive to allow this fear to immobilize our lives and cause us to remain stuck in the "status quo." On the contrary. We can use the fear and transform it into the motivation to take positive action.

First, acknowledge the fear. Trying to deny your fear will not make it go away. Accept that you have the fear and then re–focus your attention to the benefits you will gain by making the change. You can make a written list of all the good you will receive by taking action. For example, if you are going back to school (an event that can stir up a lot of old fears), focus on the new friends you will make, what you will learn and ultimately, how you will benefit by having increased your knowledge and skills.

If you want to have a successful, happy and productive life, you must learn to accept, even welcome, or embrace change. I realize this may sound strange and know it can seem difficult, but it is essential for a happy life.

We become comfortable with the status quo, going along on our path feeling fine, then suddenly — wham! — something happens to upset our apple cart. It can be something serious like the loss of a loved one, a job, or a home. It may be a minor upset like rain on your vacation or a broken date. Whatever the situation, change, or circumstance, we must learn to handle it or we may be devastated by it.

The best way I know of to deal with changing and challenging situations is to ask better questions. Ask questions like:

"How can I best cope with this situation?"

"How can I make the best of this?"

You can learn to transform your fear into power and harness that power to thrust you into a more exciting and challenging life.

Of course, it may be prudent to seek outside help, especially in serious situations. Don't be afraid to reach out for help. Our society has a support system for almost any challenge you may be facing. If all else fails, in a changing situation, remember, "This too shall pass."

GIVE YOURSELF PERMISSION TO CHANGE YOUR MIND

A reporter once asked Mother Teresa about her response to one of his questions. "Several months ago," he stated, "you said one thing and now you are saying something completely different. How do you explain the change in your position?" The saintly woman looked kindly at the man, smiled and said, "I changed my mind. I did not know then what I know now."

What a simple concept! How many of us carry around beliefs and opinions that no longer fit with who we are, simply because we have always believed them? How many times have you held onto a limiting belief because "that's the way I have always felt?"

We have been taught that being consistent and unchanging is a character attribute, whereas changing our mind is a shortcoming. We have all heard someone "stable or rock–solid" described with respect while the term "wishy washy" is used to describe one who changes their opinion.

I am challenging this concept. Sure, consistency is a character trait worth developing in certain aspects of our lives. Trustworthiness, honesty, reliability and dependability are all attributes worth striving for, however, it makes absolutely no sense to hold on to beliefs and opinions that do not serve us in the present just because they were true for us in the past. We are allowed to change our minds! As a matter of fact, if we are not changing, we are in for a real struggle. Perhaps one of the leading causes of frustration is the fact that, while we are led to believe that it is good to be consistent, the world we live in is in a state of constant change. Every part of our lives, our planet, our bodies for that matter, is in a constant state of flux while we try to resist change.

Herein lies the problem! We resist change in an ever–changing world. Resisting change in the face of a constantly changing environment has to be the height of insanity. How then can we learn to accept, even welcome, change in our lives?

One way is to look back over our lives and see that, for the most part, every change in our past has led to something better. If you do this, I think you will agree that change has been a positive force in your life.

Re–evaluate your beliefs and opinions and see if they are still true for you at this period in your growth. Considering the pace at which the world is changing; it is important to learn to embrace change in our lives.

THE BOUNCE FACTOR

Life happens. It doesn't matter how positive an attitude you have, or how balanced and centered you are, there are going to be times when you are knocked down. Times when your carefully organized life is turned upside down and you get knocked on your rear end. Life happens.

You will, no doubt, experience serious illness in either yourself or someone close to you. You may be challenged with the loss of a loved one, a divorce, the loss of a job, or any number of situations that will leave you feeling like you were kicked in the stomach. On September 11, 2001, the entire civilized world experienced this feeling.

Let's face it. These things will happen. They're part of life, and no matter how you try to explain them away with the idea that "everything happens for a reason," they hurt. A lot! They hurt at your very core. The pain begins in your heart and radiates throughout your entire being. Repeating positive phrases does not make it stop hurting.

At times like these, you're going to feel down, even depressed. You'll probably feel anger or some other manifestation of your pain. Whatever you're feeling, it's ok. It's ok to feel hurt, sad, angry, or whatever your true feelings are. You cannot deny pain any more than you can deny fear. The only way through either of these is to give yourself permission to feel the feeling.

The question isn't whether or not you will feel down. The question is how long will you stay in this state? The difference between people who get through life's challenging moments, regardless of the seriousness, and those who are immobilized by the events is what I call the Bounce factor.

How quickly can you bounce back? Of course, the severity of the event will have a lot to do with the time it will take you to get past the pain and on with your life.

This is the key. It's not whether life occasionally puts you into a tailspin, it's how long you remain there. When something devastating happens to you, allow yourself some time to grieve your loss, however, don't allow yourself to get stuck there. Take some action.

Join a support group, talk about your feelings with a trusted friend or your spiritual advisor. If necessary, seek professional help.

In the case of a job loss, perhaps you need to take some time to re-evaluate your career goals. You may even consider a change in fields.

When you're ready, you can begin networking

and making new contacts. Attend social or church events. Call people you know. Do something!

One of the most important things to remember in high stress situations is not to isolate. While spending some time alone is normal, even necessary, isolation can be dangerous and should be avoided at all costs. Get out and be with people as soon as possible. As a friend recently reminded me, "Life is for the living." It's important to get back to your life. In time, the pain will pass.

WRITE YOUR ACCOMPLISHMENTS

Several years ago, I began a practice of writing my accomplishments at the end of the year. Actually, you can do this at any time, like right now, if you've never done it.

I borrowed the idea from the corporate world. In most companies, managers are required to submit a list of their accomplishments and objectives annually. This information is used as the basis for performance reviews, raises, and promotions.

I thought, "Hey, if it works for them, maybe it will help me." The sense of personal satisfaction and encouragement I received after doing this once was so great that it has become a regular practice.

We take so much of what we do for granted, or just shrug it off, saying, "It's no big deal." We point to the successes, contributions, and accomplishments of others while overlooking all that we ourselves have done.

Only after taking the time to list our own accomplishments and activities do we see that we, too, are making a difference. We realize how much we have actually done in our lives, and this serves to motivate us to even greater heights.

In your journal, make a list of what you have done in the past year. Include everything you can think of. Where have you vacationed? What plays, movies, or concerts have you seen? What books have you read? What have you done for and with your family? What have you accomplished in your business? What about personal goals? What have you done for yourself? What about your health? Have you lost weight, began exercising, or played a sport? Did you start a business, write a book, or give a speech?

Write down everything you can think of. The more, the better. Seeing all you have done will raise your self-esteem and increase the likelihood that you will accomplish even more next year. You have probably done much more than you realize, and writing it down will enable you to see just how much you have accomplished.

KEEP AN ATTITUDE OF GRATITUDE

What are you grateful for today? If you've answered "nothing," you fall into that trap of self-pity that catches us all from time to time. We begin to look at what we don't have, and sometimes, even envy those who have more. This is one of the worst things you can possibly do. Not only does it make you feel lousy, it bores those people who happen to be around you. More importantly, it prevents good from flowing to you.

Remember, the Bible tells us, "To he who has, more is given." By focusing your attention on all the good you already possess, you create the conditions to have more good flow into your life. If you remember that what you focus on expands, then by focusing on what you already have to be grateful for, it will expand that as well.

One of the ways to remain in a positive state of mind is to develop an attitude of gratitude about your life. Whatever your present condition, there are things you can be grateful for. What about your physical and mental health? Your family and friends? Look around where you live. Consider your possessions, your job. All of those things we tend to take for granted.

Gratitude is one of the major keys to happiness. If you are feeling grateful for what you have, you will be a happy person. On the other hand, if you are constantly focusing on what you do not have, you will be miserable most of the time.

Think about all the good in your life and all that you can be grateful for: your health, your mind, your work, your family, and the fact that you live in a free country where opportunity abounds. You have your home, your friends, and the world around you. You may not know it, but you are one of the richest people in the world. Look at everything you already have. Compared to some of the world's population, if you live in North America, for example, you live like a King.

Devote some time each day to reflect on everything you are grateful for. It will immediately make you feel better. It is impossible to be grateful and feel self-pity at the same time. You will be more pleasant to be around, and people are more likely to want to be in your company. Nobody likes being around a whiner. As you do this, you will begin to attract more good into your life.

> *"There is no way to happiness.*
> *Happiness is the way"*
>
> WAYNE DYER

HAPPINESS

How many times have you said, "All I want is to be happy?" So many of us get caught up in looking outside of ourselves for happiness when, in fact, happiness is something that you can choose at any time. The old saying "Happiness is an inside job" does not refer to working indoors. It means that it is *we* who choose whether or not we are happy.

Our society has, in the past, been obsessed with using "things" in a never ending attempt to find happiness only to realize that it does not work.

Most of us just want to be happy. A wonderful spiritual study, "A Course In Miracles," says that not only should you be happy but that you should make yourself happy.

In any given situation, you can choose how you represent what is taking place. You can give away your power and let outside circumstances take away your happiness or you can claim your God given birthright to be happy and at peace, regardless of what is going on around you.

Think about it. How many times have you become unhappy because of something completely out of your control? How many times have you let other people's opinions of you, or even worse, the weather, control how you feel?

There was a time in my life when I thought that if I just bought enough "stuff", I would be happy. I thought a new car or a better stereo or bigger house would make me happy. I used to look to other people to provide the happiness that was lacking in my life. When all of that did not work and I was still not happy with myself, I was devastated. I now realize that all the material things in the world and all the other people in the world cannot, of themselves, make me happy. Only I can do that and the good part is that it does not take anything outside of myself.

> *"Eighty-five percent of life is showing up"*
> Woody Allen

Celebrate Your Life

When was the last time you actually "stopped and smelled the roses?" When was it that you stopped what you were doing long enough to see the magic of a sunset? How much of the magnificence of the world around you do you notice each day?

If you're like most people, you get caught up in your daily routines and don't always take the time to appreciate this glorious experience we call life. We all do it. We get in a rut of doing our daily tasks and busily going about our day, not even noticing the world around us. A rapid paced society is robbing us of the very stuff life is made of. Life is not about a destination, arriving, or making it. It's about the journey. It's the process of living.

Once, when I was living in southern California, a place of incredible beauty, I had become so complacent, so jaded, that I even began not to notice the majestic sunsets and beautiful sunny days. My attitude had become more like "oh yes, the sun is setting in the ocean, I saw that last week." Can you imagine taking life so much for granted?

We are born and we will die. These are absolutes. There's no way around it. We cannot change or control that fact. We can, however, make the time between these two events, whether it is a long or short time, exciting and wonderful, or we can live a life of quiet desperation. The choice is ours.

Make a habit of appreciating the world around you. Take time from your hectic schedule to see what's right in front of you. Watch children playing, birds singing, flowers blooming, and yes, the sun setting into the ocean, if you are so fortunate.

There is magic all around us. All we need do is stop and take notice. There is no charge for admission. You don't need any special equipment. The good Lord provides us with this incredible spectacle each day. All we have to do is show up for it.

AS A MAN THINKETH IN HIS HEART, SO IS HE

This idea appears in writings which date as far back as the beginning of recorded history. The same message is repeated over and over through the centuries:

"The destiny of man is in his own soul"
HERODOTES (5TH CENTURY B.C.)

"Our life is what our thoughts make of it"
MARCUS AURELIUS (121–180)

"A man's what he thinks about all day long"
RALPH WALDO EMERSON (1803–1882)

"A man is literally what he thinks"
JAMES ALLEN (1849–1925)

"We are what we believe we are"
BENJAMIN N. CARDOZO (1870–1938)

"Our self image, strongly held, essentially determines what we become"
MAXWELL MALTZ (1899–1975)

"All the resources we need are in the mind"
THEODORE ROOSEVELT (1858–1919)

Our self–talk, the constant internal dialog we have with ourselves, determines our quality of life. It is critical, therefore, to watch your every thought and word.

"If we did all the things we are capable of doing, we would literally astonish ourselves."

THOMAS A. EDISON

PLANT YOUR GARDEN

There's a saying in the computer industry, "garbage in, garbage out." It means that you get out exactly what you put in. This principle applies to our mind as well. Norman Vincent Peale, perhaps the most well known proponent of positive thinking, has said that if you remove all the negative thoughts from your mind, you must put something back in their place.

We simply cannot live in a mental vacuum. If we do not replace the negative thoughts with something positive, they will eventually return and we will slip back into our old negative thinking patterns.

As James Allen said in *As A Man Thinketh*, "A man's mind may be likened to a garden, which may be intelligently cultivated or allowed to run wild; but whether cultivated or neglected, it must and will, bring forth."

If we want our lives to remain positively directed, we must continually plant positive thoughts, affirmations and sayings on a regular basis. Perhaps this is why I am constantly reading motivational material, listening to tapes in my car, using affirmations and trying to associate with positive people in general.

I have found that the quality of my life improves in direct proportion to the amount of time I spend listening to or reading positive, uplifting material. Maybe one of the reasons I write is that I need to continually reaffirm these principles for myself. There is an old proverb that says, "We teach best what we most need to learn". If that is the case with my writing, so be it. My desired outcome is that we all benefit and grow from sharing these ideas.

As Wayne Dyer so beautifully puts it, "Everybody on the planet who is on the side of helping to improve the quality of life for all people is on my team." We are, in fact, a team.

We need to surround ourselves with people who are equally committed to personal growth. It is important to develop a network or support group of like–minded people.

With all the negativity around, it is extremely important for those of us who are trying to focus on the good and promote positive ideas, to share our experience and thoughts. This is truly a "win – win" situation.

"The Secret Of Success Is Consistency Of Purpose"
BENJAMIN DISRAELI

PURPOSE —A REASON TO EXPEND ENERGY

Many years ago I first heard that statement, and since then, I've been amazed at how often I have seen the effect of this attitude. Why, for instance, do people age differently? What keeps some people going strong well into their old age, while others seem to have given up on life and are just waiting for it to be over? I am convinced the difference is having a purpose. We need a reason to get out of bed in the morning. We need something outside of ourselves to keep us going.

There is a wonderful story about a priest who had gone to his doctor for stomach pains. The doctor informed him he had a terminal illness and suggested to the priest that he go home and put his affairs in order as he did not have long to live.

Having done this, the priest decided to make his final pilgrimage to a church he had wanted to visit in Mexico. As he was approaching the church, he saw a young boy running off with the poor box. Grabbing the youngster by the scruff of the neck, he demanded to know why he was stealing from the church. The priest learned that the boy, and many of his friends, was an orphan and had no food. He had stolen the poor box, he said, to buy something to eat. The priest was very moved by the young boy's story and went off into the village to see for himself.

To make a long story short, the priest was so moved that he began an orphanage and today, 25 years later, is still running it. He found a reason to keep going: a strong purpose in life.

How can you create a strong sense of purpose in your life? What can you do that will live on long after you've gone? Maybe it's something as simple as planting a shade tree for someone else to sit under after you've left this earth.

"It is in contrast that we find clarity"

JIM DONOVAN

WHAT DON'T YOU WANT?

While it's important to keep your attention on what you want to create in your life, something we will explore in the following pages, there is tremendous value in looking at the other side of this equation. One of the blocks to having what we want in our lives is the internal resistance that is present and operating behind the scenes.

For example, let's supposing that you want to double your current level of business. I can hear some people right now gasping at the thought of that however, it occurs all the time. This is one of the strategies I use when coaching business clients who want quantum growth.

Here's the problem; you think to yourself, "I want to double my business in the next twelve months." While you're focusing on this lofty goal, there is, in the back of your mind, all kinds of resistance to this idea. Your internal critic is chattering away telling you how difficult it will be and, even if it *were* possible, which it's not, you would have to work twice as hard and that's not something you want to do. The results here are conflicting and you are probably not even aware of it.

Fortunately, there is a fairly simple solution to this dilemma. Begin by first, identifying what you do not want. I'm not suggesting for a second that you dwell on what you don't want in your life. That will draw it to you. Just that you devote some time and energy to surface everything you don't want.

In our business doubling example, you may have things like "I don't want more work, added overhead, more debt, I don't want to have to hire more people, and I don't want to work longer, and on and on." By doing this, you've cleared the way for the next, most important step, what you do want.

Once you're clear as to what you do not want with regard to your goal or project, you can begin to list what you do want to have and experience. Again, in our business doubling example, this might include such things as "I want to double our business in the next 12 months. I want it to happen with ease and joy. I want to be able to do it with our present staff and budgets. I want it to be exciting and pleasurable for everyone. I want to be fun and have this occur effortlessly. I want to add more value to our clients. I want to explore new markets and create new ways to reach them."

By first allowing your fears and resistances to

become known to you, you've cleared the way to have more of what you do want.

Once you've identified what you don't want, don't keep going back to it. As a matter of fact, you might want to take your "don't want" list and burn it. Now devote all of your time, energy, resources, attention, thoughts, and actions to focusing on what you *do* want.

Know What You Do Want

It always puzzles me how many people have no idea what they want. In my seminars, I often ask a group of people what they want. Most of the time I get a blank stare back. Doesn't it make sense to you that knowing what you want is a prerequisite to having what you want?

In any given situation there are many possible outcomes. In business, a telephone call to a new prospective customer could result in any number of conclusions. Most likely, you want to make an appointment to see the person. If you are clear about this in the first place, your chance of succeeding is greatly increased.

While we were looking for our current home, we were having a difficult time struggling with selling one house and finding the other. One day it dawned on me that we were not focusing on our desired outcome. When we shifted our attention to what we wanted, namely the new house, everything went smoothly and we found our ideal home.

Knowing what you want in advance enables you to determine the actions that will produce your desired result. In the case of our house, what we really wanted was the new home. Once we identified this, we were able to let go of the mechanics of how the current home would be sold, and anything else that was not in line with our outcome.

By focusing our attention and efforts on locating our new home, we were able to accomplish our goal. Our other house did eventually sell, because that was part of the process that was necessary to reach our goal. The important distinction here is that our focus needed to be on the outcome, not the details.

I believe it is our job to identify what we want. Once we have done so, we are better off leaving the details in God's hands. There is no way we, from our limited perspective, can possibly know the best way for something to occur.

"Ask and it will be given to you; knock and the door will be opened to you."

MATTHEW 7:7

DREAM BIG DREAMS

Norman Vincent Peale said that if you want a big life, you need big dreams. The Bible teaches us to "ask and it will be given." Notice that it does not say "moan" or "complain." It does not advise us to settle or compromise. It says ask.

Why then do so many people settle for a life that is less than they deserve? Why do so many people settle for whatever life sends their way? Why are they afraid to dream big dreams?

Think about your own dreams. Are you holding yourself back by having dreams that are less than you really want because of some self-limiting belief about what is possible?

Instead of limiting yourself by asking for less than you really want, expand your dreams and really reach for the stars.

Think about what you really want. What kind of life would you want if there were no limits? If you could have as much money as you want, how much would that be?

Be expansive, use your imagination to dream

really big dreams. Remember that if you can dream it, you can achieve it.

Close your eyes and imagine your ideal amount of monthly income. See yourself earning this amount of money and enjoying the process. Feel what it would be like to earn this ideal amount. What would your life be like? What would you own? Where would you live? Who could you help? Who would you share your success with? In your mind, experience all of the good that would come from having this level of income.

Now, in your imagination, see yourself earning ten times this amount. How does that feel?

Did you have trouble imagining the larger amount? Most people do, until they learn to expand their sense of what is possible. Look around, are there other people earning this large amount of money? Sure there are. Then you can too. It's just a matter of believing you do deserve the life you want and being willing to make the effort to create the life you've dreamed. Dream big dreams, then go out and make them a part of your life.

You can have whatever you want if you are willing to do something in return.

"If you don't do it, you'll never know what would have happened if you had done it"

WHAT ARE YOU WAITING FOR?

"One of these days I'm going to start my own business. . . Some day I'll get around to writing a book. . . I'm going to finish my education some day. . . Some day I'll . . ."

How many times have you heard yourself repeating one of the above statements? What are you waiting for? For many people, knowing there is some life changing activity they can do and will do some day presents a false sense of security. A lot of it has to do with the fear of failure.

If a person is stuck in a job they dislike and telling themselves it's okay because one of these days they'll start their own business, they're using this as a way to justify the present situation and avoid the fear of possible failure.

Some people go through their entire lives this way. They're always telling themselves that some day they'll start whatever it is they want to begin.

The problem is that while these people are waiting for the "perfect time" to make their move, life is ticking by. This is understandable.

It's safe. It's impossible to fail if you do not actually do anything. If all you do is dream and fantasize about a business, or writing a book, or going back to school, you can't fail. You can't be rejected. You risk nothing.

Unfortunately, you can't succeed either. You'll never know what might have been unless you are willing to go ahead and actually do what it is you've always wanted to do. You owe it to yourself to do that which is burning deep within you.

> *"For of all sad words, of tongues or pen, the saddest are these: It might have been"*
>
> JOHN GREENLEAF WHITTIER (1807–1892)

DO IT NOW

Recently, someone said to me, "Yeah but I'm too old." It saddens me to hear such comments especially in light of some of the facts below, compliments of the UC Berkeley Wellness Letter.

Verdi composed his "Ave Maria" at age 85. Martha Graham performed until she was 75 and choreographed her 180th work at age 95. Michelangelo was carving the Rondanini Pieta six days before he died at 89.

Marion Hart, sportswoman and author, learned to fly at age 54 and made seven non-stop solo flights across the Atlantic, the last time in 1975 at age 83.

Grandma Moses had her first one–woman show when she was 80.

If you think you are too old to do something you've always wanted to do, you may want to reconsider and just go for it!

What is the one thing you have always wanted to do but have been putting off?

Ask yourself: "If not now, when?" Then, write your cut–off date for doing it.

DON'T DIE WITH YOUR MUSIC STILL IN YOU

The title above is a paraphrase of the Emerson quote about how "The mass of men die with their music still in them."

In light of the recent tragedy that has befallen the United States, I am sure many of us are asking the question, "If I were to die today or tomorrow, have I done what I came here to do? Have I, at least in part, 'played my special music?'"

If you answered "yes" to the question, or are at least pursuing it, then I congratulate you. If your answer is "no," I want to ask, "What are you waiting for?"

We are all special. Each of us has some special contribution to make to the world. Perhaps it's to write a book. Perhaps your special gift is in being a great teacher or coach. It could be you are the next person to discover a cure for a major disease, or to start a business and be the best you can be at what you do. Are you a builder who's passionate about your work like my friend, Tom? He sees his job as helping people achieve their lifelong dreams, and his work reflects it.

Whatever the passion within you, let it out. Life is too fragile and uncertain to postpone your dreams, hoping that "someday, I'll really begin to live my life."

Begin now! Whatever it is you're passionate about, you can begin it now. Maybe you want to do something to help your community or church group. What are you waiting for? It saddens me to see someone who is near the end their life, never having taken a step to realize their dream. It saddens me that anyone should leave this earth with their music still in them. You owe it to yourself and to humanity to let it out.

The classic poem from Johann Wolfgang Von Goethe on the opposite page is something you will want to read several times, until you feel its inspiring message deep within you. Then, make the commitment to begin your dream, acting swiftly with boldness and confidence.

UNTIL ONE IS COMMITTED,
THERE IS HESITANCY,
THE CHANCE TO DRAW BACK,
ALWAYS INEFFECTIVENESS.

CONCERNING ALL ACTS OF INITIATIVE
THERE IS ONE ELEMENTARY TRUTH,
THE IGNORANCE OF WHICH KILLS
COUNTLESS IDEAS AND ENDLESS PLANS:
THAT THE MOMENT ONE DEFINITELY COMMITS ONESELF,
THEN PROVIDENCE MOVES, TOO.

ALL SORTS OF THINGS OCCUR TO HELP ONE
THAT WOULD NEVER OTHERWISE HAVE OCCURRED.
A WHOLE STREAM OF EVENTS ISSUES FROM THE DECISION,
RAISING IN ONE'S FAVOR ALL MANNER OF
UNFORESEEN INCIDENTS AND MEETINGS AND
MATERIAL ASSISTANCE WHICH NO MAN
COULD HAVE DREAMED WOULD COME HIS WAY.

WHATEVER YOU CAN DO OR
DREAM YOU CAN, BEGIN IT!
BOLDNESS HAS GENIUS, POWER,
AND MAGIC IN IT.

JOHANN WOLFGANG VON GOETHE

CREATE A COMPELLING VISION FOR YOUR LIFE

Imagine your life being exactly the way you want it to be. How would you feel doing work you love and are passionate about? Imagine having extraordinary relationships and great friends. What would your life be like if you had all the money you want? How would you feel?

In your journal, create your vision for your ideal life. Imagine the perfect life for you. Really let go and expand your sense of what is possible. For now, forget about how. Write it all out, being sure to include the feelings associated with what you want. Feelings and emotions are the power behind being able to attract whatever you want into your life. Get your juices going. Use the questions below as a guide to help you get started.

What does this ideal vision look like?
How do you spend your time? How does it feel?
Who are your friends and associates?
How do you feel living where you live?
Where do you vacation and what do you see?
How much money do you earn?

By answering these questions in as much detail as possible, concentrating more on the feelings than the actual specifics, you will develop a clear sense of what you want your life to become. From this, you can begin to create the vision of your ideal life. Use this vision each day to put yourself in that ideal life. Read it. See it. Feel it. You will begin to attract what you want to you.

Remember, your words, thoughts and visualizations have power. We move in the direction of our currently dominant thoughts.

Devote some time each day to reading, seeing and feeling your ideal life's vision as having already occurred. Really get into the feeling associated with this ideal life. By doing this, you will begin to draw to you the very things you desire.

> *"If you don't know where you're going,
> any road will take you there"*

COMMIT YOUR
GOALS TO PAPER

It always amazes me how many people do not have written goals. Goals are critical for a successful life. In my seminars I always ask the audience to write one short-term goal that's important to them. Often I get blank looks from members of the audience. It's like they've never thought about this before. Incredible! How could you possibly have the kind of life you want if you do not know where you're going? All the success building information in the world is of no use if you do not know what you want to have happen. If you have not taken the time to identify and write your goals, how will you ever know when you are successful? Without goals, you will not recognize success when it shows up.

Take a few minutes right now to decide upon one goal for your life. I'm not asking you to do a complete goal setting session, just set one simple goal you'd like to accomplish in the next 6-12 months. Please put this book down and write in your journal, planner, or on a piece of paper, a single goal that you are committed to achieving within the next year. It may be increasing your income, starting your own business, reaching your ideal weight, spending more time with your children, or any number of things you want for your life.

Of course, if you want to set more than one goal, that's fine. But do at least one. Put a date on it and sign it.

Be sure to refer to this often and expect it to come to pass. You'll be pleasantly amazed at what will happen.

If you want to delve more into goal setting, I've written more about this in my other books, as have many others. Seek out the information you need in bookstores and libraries. Goals are simply dreams put to paper and have a way of magically coming true.

"The mass of men lead lives of quiet desperation"
HENRY DAVID THOREAU

SET MINI GOALS

Hopefully you have completed the previous exercises and are using your ideal vision and goal setting as a way of guiding your life in the direction you want it to go.

This is the single, most important aspect of personal development, and one that can make the difference between a life of prosperity, happiness, health, abundance, love, passion, joy and more, and a life, as Thoreau said, of quiet desperation.

Mini, or incremental, goals are somewhat different in that they break a larger goal down into its smallest part. A mini goal might be a daily goal that is part of a larger, more expansive goal you're working on.

For example, if one of your goals is to improve your health, your mini goal could be to exercise and eat low fat meals just for today. You can then reward yourself for having reached your daily goal. This will further reinforce your determination and resolve, helping you to stick to your plan and move toward your larger health goals.

Many highly successful salespeople set daily

and weekly sales goals and magically exceed their monthly and yearly quotas by focusing on the smaller, mini goals. Doing this on a daily basis will automatically move you closer to your big goals while rewarding you with successes along the way.

At the beginning of your week, think about what you want to accomplish for that period. Set some mini goals for yourself for the week ahead. You can break these down even further into daily goals. Decide what daily actions you will take to move you toward your bigger goals. This small investment of time spent planning will result in big rewards in your productivity.

*God is the creator, the mind is the builder,
the physical is the result.*

LEARN TO VISUALIZE

Whatever you can vividly imagine, you can achieve. Everything in your world and everything around you was once an idea in the mind of its inventor or creator.

Invest time each day visualizing what you want in your life. Sit quietly in a place where you will not be disturbed. The best time to do this is just before going to sleep at night and just upon awakening in the morning. Close your eyes and take a few deep breaths. Relax. Become quiet and at peace. Mentally create a picture of what you want. See it as vividly as you can. Don't strain. Add color and sound and smells. Engage all of your senses.

You may even want to picture a movie screen in your mind's eye and project your image onto the screen. Just relax and see this picture. Don't worry if it's not a perfect picture. What matters is that you are teaching your subconscious mind what you want to have in your life.

If you want to lose weight and be in better health, see yourself as the person you want to become. If you want a new house, picture it in your mind's eye. See the rooms and property. What does the kitchen look like? How about the master bedroom? What is the view from the living room window? What about the den? Add as much detail as you can.

After a few minutes of this, say to yourself, "all of this and more is my divine right," or some other closing prayer or affirmation. Doing this for ten or fifteen minutes each day will help you stay on track and will bring into play the powers of your subconscious mind to help you reach your goal.

Relax and have fun with it. Remember the story of the opening day of Disney World in Orlando, when the reporter exclaimed to Walt's brother, Roy, "It's too bad Walt didn't live to see this." Roy, without missing a beat said, "Walt saw it first, that's why you're seeing it now."

> *"The future belongs to those who believe
> in the beauty of their dreams."*
>
> ELEANOR ROOSEVELT

SEE YOURSELF AS THE PERSON YOU'RE BECOMING

Do you carry around a mental image of yourself as overweight and unhealthy, when you really want to be fit, trim and in radiant health? Do you have an internal image of yourself as broke, never having enough money, when your heart's desire is to be rich and prosperous? Do you affirm disliking your job and not being able to get ahead, when you really want your own business where you call the shots?

Then, my friend, you must change your mental image of yourself. You must begin to see yourself as the person you want to become. Affirm the characteristics and lifestyles of the person you want to be.

All change begins in your mind. Before you can change your circumstances you must first imagine yourself differently.

Begin to think, talk, and act as the person you want to become. Doing that in the present will move you toward your future lifestyle. For example, if the person you want to become is trim and healthy, the next time you encounter a dessert tray at a restaurant ask yourself, "What would this healthy, new me do in this situation?" Chances are you'll pass it by.

If you want to become a more understanding and loving parent, the next time one of your children does something that makes you angry, behave as the person you are working toward becoming would behave in the same situation.

One of the ways in which we sabotage ourselves is to carry around old pictures in our minds and replay old tapes that undermine our progress. If you want to become wealthy, stop seeing yourself as broke or poor. Stop affirming lack and talking about not having enough money. Stop complaining about your bills. A wealthy person would not do these things.

One of the "secrets" to becoming wealthy is to affirm wealth. Express your gratitude for all that you already have. Count your blessings. No matter how broke or "poor" you may think you are, if you live in the United States you are better off than most of the world's population. By affirming your present wealth, health, and opportunities, you are creating a mental state that will attract more. Remember, "to he who has, more is given."

Make a habit of acting, thinking, visualizing, and talking as the person you would like to become. The more you do this, the faster you will move toward this goal.

*"Our prayers are answered not when we're given
what we ask, but when we are challenged
to be what we can become."*

MORRIS ADLER

BRIDGING THE GAP
OF UNCERTAINTY

If you've ever been driving along an icy road and gone into a skid, you know what I'm referring to as the "Gap of Uncertainty." It's that moment, which can seem like an eternity, between the time you turn the steering wheel to counter the skid and the time the car actually follows. Racing car drivers understand this all too well, and know that no matter what, they must not take their eyes away from the direction they want to go. They know that if they just have faith, everything will turn out fine. If they give in to their fears and look toward the skid, they'll spin out and crash.

We are very often faced with the same situation in our lives. We complete our goal setting exercises, clearly identifying our deepest desires, write them in our journals, and begin taking action toward their accomplishment. However, there is a time gap, the "gap of uncertainty," between when we begin to see ourselves differently and when these inner visions manifest in the material world.

For example, you may be seeing yourself as financially successful and behaving as if you have achieved your goal - thinking about, acting, and affirming your prosperity - while in reality, you are still trying to make ends meet. Does this mean you have failed? Of course not! It is simply the gap of time that it takes for your inner visions to become your outer reality. It means that you must call upon your faith and inner strength to stay focused on your goals and believe they will appear.

It is a universal law that whatever you hold in your mind and thoughts, consistently, will come to pass. The Bible says that whatever you ask for in prayer, believe you have received it, and it will be given unto you. The operative word here is believe. Your unswerving faith in your ability to achieve your goals and create the life you desire, energizes your personal power, thereby creating the magnetism that will draw them to you.

Stay focused on your most important goals. Continue to affirm and have faith that they are, indeed, coming to you, staying alert to opportunities that are around you.

During this Gap of Uncertainty, do not become discouraged and think you have failed. Simply realize this is part of the process and have faith that your life is changing, knowing that what you keep uppermost in your consciousness will take form in your reality. Continue to visualize your goals as having already been achieved. Verbally affirm your intention in everything you say and do, and most of all, do not give up.

CELEBRATE YOUR VICTORIES

For years, whenever I reached a goal I would simply cross it off my list and set a new one. Then one day I read a suggestion from Mark Victor Hansen, co–author of Chicken Soup for the Soul. He suggested celebrating your victories. Instead of crossing off a goal you've reached, put a star next to it or a big, brightly colored "V" for Victory. You could even put it on your wall on your treasure map.

I have a large poster board in my office that I use to post items that remind me of my progress. This serves me well as a place to put pictures of what I want to attract into my life, as well as goals that I want to achieve and goals that I have already accomplished.

I've recently added a second board to hold the many letters that I receive from readers. This is a constant reminder to me of why I'm doing what I do. For me, there is absolutely nothing so gratifying as knowing that someone has been helped by something I wrote.

Create your own victory wall to hold evidence of your successes. It will help you stay focused and motivated, especially on those days that are "less than great."

The more you celebrate reaching your goals, the more motivated you will become to stretch even further and reach new heights. Each goal you reach will encourage you to stretch yourself even further and set bigger goals. Stretching yourself is what makes your life magical. You'll never know what you are capable of accomplishing until you stretch.

Each new accomplishment serves as a reminder of how far you've come in your journey. By keeping a record of the goals you've reached, you constantly reinforce your belief in your ability to accomplish what you want for your life.

> *"If you believe, you will receive whatever you ask for in prayer"*
>
> MATTHEW 21:22

THE POWER OF QUESTIONS

This is perhaps the single most powerful strategy I have ever learned. Master this and you will take control of your life.

If you can learn to formulate self–empowering questions and apply their answers, you can improve your condition and speed up your progress in any area of your life.

If you stop and think about it, we are constantly asking ourselves questions. What I am suggesting here is to consciously choose empowering questions rather than dis–empowering ones.

Too many people sabotage their progress and growth by asking what I like to refer to as "stupid questions." These are the closed loop questions we ask ourselves. We ask things like: "why me?" or "why can't I lose weight, get a better job, get a date" or whatever it is we are trying to do.

This establishes two conditions that undermine our well–being. First, we automatically establish that we are never able to do whatever it is we want to accomplish. Second, it just keeps our mind going around in circles looking for an answer. There is no answer to this type of question. That is the problem.

A more self–empowering approach might be to rephrase the question. For example, if you want to lose weight, you could ask: "What actions can I take to reach my ideal weight?" or, to make it an even better question, "How can I reach my goal weight and enjoy the process."

Questions such as these, when used on a consistent basis, will cause our mind to seek solutions rather than go in circles. In the Bible it says: "Ask and you shall receive" it does not say "whine" or "demand." It says Ask!

We are conditioned to answer questions. Do you agree? Do you disagree? Whatever your response, you had to ask yourself a question to determine your position. If someone asks you if you know the time, chances are you will answer them. It is human nature.

What I am suggesting is that we use this approach to assist us in our everyday lives.

I have used this technique successfully many times. A word of caution: be patient. If you keep asking positive, self–empowering questions, you will get answers.

If you, like so many people, want to go into your own business but do not know what kind, try asking yourself the following:

"What do I love to do?"
"What would I do if I knew I could not fail?"
"What would I do even if I were not paid for it?"
"How can I do that and make it profitable?"

You may be pleasantly surprised at the result. In your journal, write one question to help you with an issue in your life. As the answers come, write them down. You can even do this on a daily basis. You will be amazed at all the good answers that come to you over a period of time.

For even greater results, use this technique along with your goal setting and vision exercises. Keeping in mind your main goals, formulate a question relating to their achievement. For example, if you want freedom and financial independence, you can ask: "What can I do that will make me financially independent while giving me the freedom to do what I love?"

Each day, ask the question and then spend some time writing the answers you receive from your sub–conscious mind. Over time, you will have a significant number of good ideas, any one of which can change your life.

MODEL SUCCESS

Perhaps the most powerful strategy for success, and the least used, is a technique called modeling.

Simply put, it means locating someone who has successfully achieved the result you wish to achieve, finding out what they did, and doing it. If you model someone's beliefs, actions, and strategies you will produce the same result they did.

For example, let us suppose you want to shed 50 pounds. Before going on yo-yo diets and starving yourself, you can eliminate a lot of the time, pain, and frustration simply by finding someone who has successfully lost a significant amount of weight and kept it off.

Question them as to their beliefs. What do they tell themselves? Find out about their actions. What exactly did they do? What is their strategy for successfully keeping the weight off?

If you then go out and duplicate their process, you will achieve the same or a similar result. After all, we are not all that different. We all have similar physical, emotional, mental, and neurological systems that respond in pretty much the same way.

When I recently found myself gaining too much weight, a problem I've struggled with for years, I decided I needed to find a permanent solution. I had tried every diet and health program and read most of the books written on the subject. Several had worked for a period of time, but sooner or later, the weight crept back on. The problem was that all these diets, while nutritionally sound, had lists of foods I could no longer eat. I'm sure it's no great surprise to you that these were also some of my favorite foods. For me, this kind of program will not work long term. Sure, I can stop eating almost any food for a period of time, but for the rest of my life? I don't think so! I enjoy food and dining in fine restaurants is one of my favorite pleasures. I needed to find a program I could follow for the rest of my life.

After watching several close friends, including my wife, reach their weight goals on the Weight Watcher program, I joined the group. One of the things that drew me to this particular program is that it is not a diet, but rather, a weight management program. It's fairly simple to follow, and within reason, allows me to eat whatever foods I enjoy. I now have a strategy I can use to help me maintain my ideal weight and still enjoy eating for the rest of my life.

Perhaps you have recently begun your own business. Seek out the top people in your industry and ask them how they do it. My experience has been that truly successful people are usually more than willing to tell you their "secret." After all, they most likely had someone help them in the beginning. If the person you ask is, for some reason, not willing to help you, ask someone else. By modeling the successful strategies of those who have gone before, you will shortcut the entire process and save yourself a lot of bumps, bruises, and setbacks.

Whatever results you are seeking, whether it's health, wealth, learning, relationships, spirituality, or anything else, there are people who know the formula for success. It makes sense to avail yourself of their experience and willingness to help.

BE CAREFUL WHOSE ADVICE YOU'RE TAKING

Have you ever noticed that there is no shortage of people willing to give you advice, whether or not you asked for it?

I've developed some simple rules about from whom I will accept advice and suggestions. I do not ask for heath advice from people who are sick, I do not ask for financial advice from people who are broke, and I do not ask for business advice from people who are not in their own business.

Over the years, I've watched hundreds of people go into a business venture and excitedly tell their family and friends about their new enterprise. Big mistake, unless of course, they're in business. If you want advice or input about a business, find someone who is successfully running their own business and ask them. Ask several people so you can obtain an objective view.

When you're choosing mentors or role models, be sure to seek out those people who have been there. Chose people who have "walked the walk" and have succeeded in doing what you want to do. This applies as much to health, finance, education, relationships, and pretty much any area of your life.

If you want to be fit and healthy, do not seek advice from someone who is overweight, a smoker, and sick all the time. Find a fit and healthy person and model them.

I know this sounds overly simple and obvious, but it never ceases to amaze me how many people are listening to, and even following, the advice of people who do not know what they are talking about.

They are, unfortunately, listening to the person who is stuck in a dead-end job telling them why a business idea will not work. They are listening to an overweight, sick person who is telling them that taking vitamins is a waste of money, and they are listening to the person who is living paycheck to paycheck telling them how to become wealthy.

To guarantee your success, make sure your role models are demonstrating, in their own lives, the qualities you seek to develop.

GIVING BACK

In addition to you and your family enjoying the fruits of your labor, make a habit of giving back. One of the greatest feelings of personal satisfaction comes from being able to give to others, especially those who are less fortunate. There are many ways you can use your wealth to enrich your community, your spiritual community, and the people who need a helping hand. There is an added pay-back for you in that it is virtually impossible to give without receiving.

The practice of tithing is written about in every book on success and spirituality and is a universal law. Tithing a percentage of your income, usually 10%, to your church or other spiritual organization not only helps that group but sends a signal to your subconscious that you are wealthy enough to afford to do this, thus reinforcing your prosperity mind set.

Many people have the attitude that they will tithe when they, themselves, have more. This is backwards. If you follow the teachings of the great religions and teachers throughout history, you will learn that the best time to begin tithing is when you yourself are in need. This opens the flow of good toward you. Besides, it's a lot easier to make a habit of tithing if you begin with small amounts. The wealthier you are, the larger the amount of your tithe and the harder it is to write the check. If you doubt this, imagine how it feels to tithe ten percent of a thousand dollars. Easy enough, right? You just write a $100 check.

Now, imagine tithing the same ten percent but this time imagine the amount to be one hundred thousand dollars. The check you'd be writing would then be $10,000. Which would you find easier to give away?

It is a universal law that as you give, so shall you receive. Consequently, it is impossible to give unconditionally and not receive. As a matter of fact, you receive more than you give.

The Bible talks about receiving tenfold, so you cannot lose. This is an amazing principle, and one that anyone, regardless of their situation in life, can employ.

You can always give something. Love, time, money, labor, material goods, and even an act of simply giving a little of your time to help another will bring you untold rewards.

I'm not talking about giving with expectations or doing good deeds for personal gain. I'm suggesting that you can give freely of yourself, your money, and your time, knowing that whatever you need will be returned to you in some way.

Giving and helping one another is one of the most rewarding things we can do. It returns to us a sense of personal satisfaction and good feelings that money cannot buy. It is our nature to give and to serve. We are here to give and to help each other.

I was once asked if I knew how much money billionaire J. Paul Getty left when he died. When I said I did not know, my friend replied, "All of it."

You see, we are taking nothing with us when we pass, except our good deeds. To me, this simple fact is proof that we are here to give and serve. Otherwise, we would be able to take our possessions with us when we die.

"I am still learning"
MICHAELANGELO

BECOME A LIFELONG LEARNER

Invest ten or fifteen minutes each day reading self-help, inspirational books, or books about your areas of interest. If you make this one simple change, you will have spent over fifty hours a year learning new information. That's a lot of learning for only a ten or fifteen minute investment. In five or ten years, by investing just a few minutes each day, you could be a world class expert.

Imagine if you turned your car radio off, and instead, listened to information on educational cassette tapes while driving. For some, this would mean a couple of hours a day taking in new information. That would add up to over five hundred hours of learning in just one year.

Too many people stop learning the day they graduate from school. Instead, they waste precious reading time on newspapers, gossip magazines, and romance novels. In their cars, they sing along with the latest hit songs. I'm not suggesting you stop this altogether, but simply that you use some of your reading and commuting time to work on your own development.

We live in a rapidly changing world and it's becoming necessary to keep pace with the change while constantly upgrading our skills. The workplace no longer offers lifetime job security. Instead, it offers the most desirable, high paying positions to those people who bring the best skills to the company. You can no longer rely on the company to train you and help you upgrade your capabilities. It is up to you. If you're in business, it's up to you to stay on top of the latest innovations and changes taking place in your industry.

Some time ago, I learned of a strategy that one of the most successful direct sales companies in the world uses to develop new representatives and help them succeed. They encourage their people to invest ten to fifteen minutes a day reading self-help books. This translates to about a book a month or twelve books a year.

I began following this suggestion myself. What I learned was very interesting and enlightening. On the days that I read, my attitude and overall experiences were better than the days I did not read. The brief period of time spent reading would leave me in a more positive, optimistic frame of mind with which to begin my day.

Make a commitment now to invest time each day reading and listening to tapes.

TAKE TIME OUT TO PLAY

As they say, all work and no play makes Jack and Jill a very dull boy and girl. We all need time to relax and just "play." No matter how much you truly love and enjoy your work, from time to time it is necessary to just get away from it all. This may mean going on a trip, if only for a day or two, or an extended vacation of several weeks. Perhaps, for you, it means staying put right where you are, but taking time away from your day to day work to get out and see what the rest of the world looks like.

Believe it or not, doing this can be the best business strategy you have, especially if you're stuck in a rut. Removing yourself from the day-to-day routines associated with running your business, or household, helps clear your mind and opens it to new ideas and possibilities. It takes you out of your patterned behavior and stimulates your creativity by presenting you with new experiences, sights, and sounds, and new stimuli to awaken your creativity.

We tend to become stuck in our daily routines, like driving the same path to and from work, seeing the same sights, walking the same route when we exercise, and even eating essentially the same foods on a regular basis. Most of us eat the same eight to ten foods from the hundreds available to us in your average grocery store. We begin to live on "auto pilot" and the creative side of our brain tunes out and goes to sleep.

By breaking our routines and disrupting our patterns, we bring new sensations into our minds. Our creative, right brain hemisphere perks up and begins creating again. Every book ever written about becoming more creative talks about changing our behavioral patterns as one way to jump-start our creative juices.

Being away from your everyday environment gives you the opportunity to see life in other locations. Whenever I travel, I make a point of observing what local businesses are doing. I usually talk to one or two business people in the town or city I'm visiting. This gives me a totally new perspective and opens my thinking to new possibilities.

Simply being in an unfamiliar location causes us to think and act differently. It takes us out of our routines, moves us away from our comfort zone, and literally bombards our creative minds with new and exciting sights and sensations.

Take time to play. Not only will you return more relaxed and rested, you'll undoubtedly have new ideas and a renewed enthusiasm for your life.

TOLERATE NOTHING

In closing, I'd like to leave you with a thought and a suggestion. As the title of one of my books points out, "This is your life, not a dress rehearsal." You deserve the best life has to offer.

This means having a life where you feel safe in your own home. A life where you are treated well and respected by others. A life that is free from the things you do not wish to experience.

In the field of professional coaching, there is something called *Tolerations*. These are the things that, for whatever reason, you tolerate in your life. Sometimes, they're minor inconveniences like a friend who's always late for appointments. Sometimes, people tolerate serious things like physical or emotional abuse. You do not have to tolerate that which you do not want to have in your life.

Take some time to look at your life as it is right now. What are you tolerating that you'd rather be rid of? Do you tolerate friends who constantly put you down? Why? Why not surround yourself with people who will support you in your endeavors, whatever they may be. After all, it's your life, isn't it? Do you tolerate a boss who treats you poorly? No one should have to put up with disrespect. Maybe you should have a talk with this person and let them know how you feel. Perhaps, it's time to look for another position or a career change.

Do you tolerate an abusive parent, spouse or child? Don't! Go and get some help before it's too late. Help is there if you reach out for it.

What about your home? Are you tolerating a dirty, cluttered environment when what you really want is a clean, uncluttered one? Change it! Do you tolerate an automobile that runs poorly or is unsafe? Have it fixed!

What are you tolerating in your health? Do you tolerate being overweight and in poor health when you'd really rather be healthy & fit?

It's your life and it's up to you to make it what you want it to be. Tolerate nothing. You are in control. This is your life, not a dress rehearsal.

CONCLUSION

Congratulations! You are on your way to reclaiming your life. If you've read this far, you've probably realized that lasting happiness and an exciting life are not so much a matter of learning some new idea or making some huge change. It's the small changes we make in our attitudes and behaviors. It's the small changes we make in our day-to-day lives and our daily actions. It's the small changes we make to take back our power and create the lives we were born to live.

If you want to continue to grow and experience your life at the highest possible level, I suggest you continue reading books like this, listen to personal growth tapes in your car or while exercising, and attend as many seminars and talks as you possibly can. Keep a journal of your ideas, goals, and feelings. It's a great way to track your progress and record your life as you live it.

Make a habit of reading something uplifting and inspirational each day. It is our daily actions that will create our experiences and shape our destiny.

Most importantly, have fun. Be gentle with yourself. You do not have to be perfect. Lighten up! Learn to relax and wear your life as a loose fitting garment.

Above all, live your life with passion. Get excited about creating your life. Learn to fully experience the world you live in. Be kind to those you encounter on your journey through life. Most of all be kind and gentle with yourself.

I am honored you have chosen to read this book and wish you the very best of happiness and success in your life.

If you'd like to continue to receive ideas from me, be sure to subscribe to my free email newsletter. Simply visit my Web site at www.jimdonovan.com.

Be well, and may God bless you,

Jim Donovan

Buckingham, Pennsylvania

ABOUT THE AUTHOR

Jim Donovan, a native New Yorker, has implemented the timeless principles in his books to first turn his own life around, and then to devote his life to helping others do the same. Jim practices these principles every day and is living proof that they work. An author, coach, and highly sought after inspirational speaker he has touched the hearts of thousands of people, just like you, who have wanted a better life. Crossing all age and gender barriers, his simple message has been embraced by teenagers and seniors alike. From CEO's to single parents, people are improving the quality of their lives by following his simple truths.

Other books by Jim Donovan

Handbook to a Happier Life
This is Your Life, Not a Dress Rehearsal

Available in book stores or at
www.jimdonovan.com.

Visit www.jimdonovan.com to sign up for a free subscription to the Jim's Jems e-zine for personal and professional growth. Published since 1991, Jim's Jems is read by individuals and business people throughout the world.

Inquire about having Jim Donovan as a guest speaker for your next event.

Learn more about working with Jim as your personal coach or for your business.

Find out how your business can obtain copies of this book for your own employees, to use at trade shows or to sponsor copies to be donated, in your name, to those in need.

Or, for any other information, please call (215) 794-3826 or email jim@jimdonovan.com.